D1327159

PLEASE TO BEGIN

PLEASE TO BEGIN

By Jim Metcalf

Photographs by Sonny Carter

PELICAN PUBLISHING COMPANY
GRETNA 1976

Copyright © 1976 by James M. Metcalf
All rights reserved
ISBN: 0–88289–140–5

Manufactured in the United States of America

Published by Pelican Publishing Company, Inc.
630 Burmaster Street, Gretna, Louisiana 70053

Library of Congress Cataloging in Publication Data

Metcalf, Jim.
  Please to begin.

  I. Title.
PS3563.E817P55   811'.5'4   76–26923
ISBN 0–88289–140–5

Contents

PLEASE TO BEGIN

Winter Visitor

If the time of April
were upon us,
you'd be just another day—
so much like the ones
that came before you
and the ones that would come after—
that your loveliness would go unnoticed
in the sameness of a springtime sequence,
when beauty follows beauty
from sun to moon to sun again.

But now, in winter,
you violate the mandates
of a calendar that dictates
what your nature ought to be . . .
and your warm kiss
is made the sweeter
when felt on cheeks
that recall the touch of winter . . .
just a day ago.

And the song you sing
of summer things,
reminds us
that the bleakest winter passes . . .
and that to sleep
is not to die.

Flock of Gulls

Swirl upward from the sea
like clouds of leaves
on anxious autumn winds
hurrying to erase
the final trace of summer.

Fly as free
as children's souls
are free . . .
as wide as the sea is wide.

Head out
to where the sea and sky
are one . . .
    and on the way,
    look back
and call a mourning call
for me . . .
a prisoner
with chains that bind me
to the shore.

Fog

Softly,
with a silken cutting edge,
the fog descends
and quietly decapitates
the towers that surround us.

Like Sleepy Hollow's headless ghost
they stand,
fading out of sight
into a limbo world
somewhere between earth and heaven.

And inside,
eyes through windows see
different versions of reality . . .
            depending on their point of view . . .
            the level of the window that they choose
            to look out and see it through.

Skyline

The dusk turns on the colored lights
and leaves the profile of the city
stuck against a pink and purple limbo
like black construction paper,
cut just so.
> Scissors with rounded points,
> little kids
> with little red tongues
> in mouth corners,
> cutting,
> gluing,
> crayolaing a poster:
> "BEAUTIFY OUR CITY WEEK."

Regard the levels, children—
and the tiers
and the sudden jumps of man-made peaks.

Just the profile, please.
From a distance, please.
It's prettier that way . . .
> without the people showing.

Exodus

Another year is ending.
The pieces of the final days
are crumbling down.
Their hours and their minutes
melted
by the ceaseless tides of time,
they slip silently
        into the sea of memories
        that claims all our yesterdays.

And now,
in the impatient interim
between the wilting
of the Christmas tree
and the new year soon to be,
we wait . . .
        for endings
        and for beginnings.

But there will be neither.
Nothing will be changed,
save for a number.

The sun will rise and set
the same.
The winds will blow
and rivers flow,
    and seasons will give way to seasons
    as God will have them do.

And life will be
as it has always been—
    cycles within a circle,
    whirling
    without starts or finishes,
    through the timeless places
      of forever.

Clouds

The clouds,
like painted dreams of poets' souls,
roam the prairies of the sky.
They rise and fall
and billow and run,
free from the chains that bind us
to a world of limitations.

Yet,
they, too, have masters
that must be served.
They, too,
have their chains.
They go where they are told to go . . .
and when.

They can travel
no faster than the wind . . .
no higher than the air . . .
no lower than the sea.

Their freedom is, like ours,
a passing, sometimes thing—
a respite
now and then,
from the dictates of
a universe of law.

A Thank You Note on Father's Day for Marc, Michael, Jamie, and Clare

The gifts were lovely. I shall keep and cherish them forever—and I thank you for them. However, I have so much more to thank you for . . . gifts you have given me each day of your lives without ever knowing it.

I thank you for what you have made of me. For even with all my frailties and shortcomings, I would be much less a man without you.

You have made me stronger by putting me in situations that demanded strength, and though many times I wanted to turn my back and walk away, you would not let me. You looked to me in your helplessness and made me do what I had to do, and whether it was right or wrong, I acted, and grew stronger by it.

You have made me wiser by challenging my beliefs and causing me to question them. And some of them could not stand the test of closer scrutiny . . . the tracing of their origins . . . so they were discarded and with them went some hate . . . some prejudices I had not recognized as such before. And I am more tolerant without them.

You have made me less selfish. You have taught me how to WANT to give. Taught me that party dresses at a certain age are more important than three hundred dollar suits to impress a client. That footballs and baseballs and flutes and clarinets and college books and gasoline for klunkers are more important than savings bonds for retirement years.

I would never have believed all that before I came to know the four of you.

I thank you for showing me a kind of love I could not have known without you. And I grow cold when I think of all I would have missed.

My God . . . what I would have missed.

Sea Birds

Lonely,
and wondering
if you've gone for good,
I stood
and watched the sea birds
fly in before the sun today,
pulling summer
on a leash of cotton cloud
behind them.

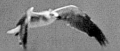

One sweep they made
across the beach,
then back to sea again.

They've brought our lovely
bronze and azure season home.

Maybe they'll come back
tomorrow . . .
and maybe
they'll bring you.

Our Last Goodbye

Promise me
that when our time together
has been spent—
    when we say our last goodbye—
if you are left
to keep the memory
of what we felt
and what we were
and the beauty of our love,
    you will not cry.

For parting is the price
we pay for loving—
a pittance
    for so wondrous a thing.

Seasons bloom
and seasons die
and nights chase days
across the sky.
    For every first hello
    there is a last goodbye.

But for us,
the time between the two
has made it all worthwhile.
So remember
every precious day of it
and don't cry,
but smile.

Once in April

Once in April,
        running
through the meadows
of a timeless time,
I believed the promise
of a newborn season . . .
an eternity
of youth and spring.

Then in September,
        walking
in a quiet and wooded place
where trees stood
draped in sacrificial red and gold,
I felt the coming
of a somber season
and the sun was growing dim.

Now in December,
        sitting
by a fire,
I look out my window
at a barren land
I never saw before.

Where are the meadows
of that other time?
Where
the splendid shades of Autumn?

Somewhere,
across the way . . .
beyond the forest
still and gray,
another Spring lies sleeping,
waiting for its day.

But it will not be mine.
For my years now
belong to Winter.
I've left my Aprils
far behind.

Don't Pity Me My Years

I hope I don't see pity
in the young and eager eyes
I love,
when they look upon my face
someday
and see my years imprinted there—
    Wrinkles
they don't remember seeing
the last time that we met . . .

    A smile
that's not as ready,
not as quick . . .
    Eyes
that seem a little dimmer . . .
    A certain hesitation
when I speak.

Feel sadness,
if you must, my loves,
because our time together
soon will end.

But please don't pity me my years.
My beautiful,
my precious years . . .
my treasures every one . . .
my wealth . . .
my sustenance
for all the days to come.

No matter what the future holds,
how bleak the circumstance,
nothing can destroy
the joy
that I have known.

      I have lived
      and I have won.
      Life cannot cheat me now.

So, don't pity me my years,
my loves . . .
for I do not envy you
your youth.

Anniversary

The January day they were married
had been a cold, grey extension
of the night that came before it.
The sun had battled with the clouds—
had lost—
and now lay dying in a shroud of fog
above an invisible horizon.
And as they were walking
through the park,
the day became the night again,
and they never knew the difference.
They were in love,
and they made times and seasons
of their own.
They commanded suns and moons,
and it was warm or cold
or dawn or dusk,
as they would have it be.

But even with their powers,
they couldn't stop the years from passing.
And one day, they grew old.

Now, looking out a window
at young lovers,
laughing in the snow,
they wonder
how they keep so warm
in January's cold.

And I Will Meet Tomorrow

Across the way,
beyond the rooftops
and the trees,
the light surrenders wearily
to the darkness.
And quietly, another day is taken
from my allotted number.

Yet, the loss is made to seem
no loss at all
by the beauty
that surrounds its dying.
Wrapped in hues and colors,
not of death,
but brilliant shades of promise
and fulfillment . . . .
Pledges made in blue and gold
that there will be tomorrows,
clean, untouched . . .
as good or bad as I will have them be.

So I will not mourn
this day that dies at eventide.
I will let it take its place
with my other yesterdays.
And I will wait the darkness through,
and then
I will meet tomorrow.

The Library

Do the children still come here
as once we did
so long ago,
        to search,
        to dream,
        to find new worlds
they never knew existed?

Do they still fall in love
        with books?
Do they know
        their feel,
        their smell,
        their sound
when pages turn?
. . . like wind through autumn trees . . .

Have they shared
long winter afternoons
        and nights
        by hidden candlelight
        in quiet houses,
when all others were asleep?

Do they know of pirate ships
        with skull and crossbones
        flying . . .
        and stormy midnight
        horseback rides
to save the settlement
from dying?

And do they know
the craft men flew
        to reach the stars,
        long before the Astronauts
        were dreamed of?

All this we saw
        and heard,
        and felt,
in dimensions greater far
than moving shadows
        behind a pane of glass
        on an electronic improbability.

Do they still read . . . the children?
        Do they still
        know how?

Anchorman

Skipping through fields
of eggshell egos,
where the promise
of sudden fame goes,
he goes,
oblivious of whatever ties there be
that bind him to mediocrity.
Polishing the tools to carve his niche,
    (statements platitudinous,
    interpretations latitudinous)
all carefully intoned . . . falsetto rich.
With show biz cunning
and tutored wile,
covering ignorance
with a sexy smile.

Packaged in his hand— the world,
the ludicrous, the tragic,
shredded and baled
by electronic magic.

The king is on the throne.
The king is hailed.
(CUE THE KING!)

"Good evening . . .
17 ginglegarbs have cravvergasted
an oskolometer from the Frankensmuck
cornerstaff . . . More slakorbens after
this brief rennipuff."

In Parting

Goodbye,
sweet, gentle lover.
We shall not meet again.
The fever of our interlude
is over,
but we each have gained
a friend.
Goodbye,
sweet, gentle friend.
    May the songs you sing
    be happy ones . . .
    and the voices that you hear
    be filled with joy.
    May you walk through friendly meadows,
    flower bright
    and sunshine warm.
    May the hands of loved ones
    be close by
    to brush away the tears
    if you should cry.
        And someday,
        may you find the peace
            that only you
                can bring you.

Diary on the River

(Notes made while traveling from Natchez, Mississippi to New Orleans on the paddle-wheeler "Natchez" . . . Autumn of 1976)

It's noon now and the shoreline is still much as it has been since we left Natchez at dawn today . . . wild and undeveloped . . . like it must have been back in the 1800s, and I feel that maybe yesterday is hiding just around the bend and that I might pass right through it and never even know. There is nothing on either side to tell me what century I am in.

But suddenly, it is unmistakably today. Through a narrow clearing in the trees I see the sun reflected in the windshield of a speeding car, racing down some hidden highway. Above, a rope of white trails out behind a jet, unravels and stretches out of sight across the sky.

And yesterday is left behind . . . somewhere up the river.

But somehow, time doesn't seem as important when reckoned from the river. There is a sort of detached objectivity here.

A feeling that what is happening on the shores that line my way is not of my concern, for I am no part of it.

A feeling that I am merely an observer . . . impartial and uninvolved . . . passing *through* time and change, untouched by either . . . moving ever closer to the journey's end—the foreverness of the sea.

A Deeper Shade of Purple

The night is almost here.
There's room for just
one deeper shade of purple
to be spread between the layers
of the darkness and the light—
time for one last farewell glance
at the silhouette that was today.

How soon grown old . . .
How soon to die . . .
How little time
to find an antidote
for the ugliness it brought.

Yet, I cannot let it die this way.
Please let it show me
something beautiful
before it goes.

Not as much to please my senses
as to reassure my soul.

Suddenly, across the darkening way,
I see a field of yellow flowers sway.
White curtains on my window
flirt shamelessly
with a passing summer breeze,
and the sweet, sweet smell of clover
fills my room.

The lights in town are coming on
and up and down the street,
I hear mothers' voices
calling children home . . .
echoes from another time.

       And now it ends.

The day has died in beauty.
My soul will be at peace.
       And I will lay me down to rest . . .
       And I will lay me down
         to sleep.

Imperfections

Now it was ending . . .
this marriage that was,
like those who brought it into being,
so young . . . so very young.
It was dying in the afternoon
of a December day,
quietly,
in the cold of a harsh, unfeeling season.
And that day of sun and flowers
and bands of gold
and words, soft spoken
in a tiny chapel
when April was outside,
meant less than nothing now.

And they did not know
why it was happening as it was.
They could not say when or where
it started . . .
or how it grew
and led to this . . . .
It just hadn't worked out
the way they thought it would,
they said.

It just hadn't worked out.
And there was no bitterness . . .
no hate . . . .
It was, they said,
by mutual agreement.
They did not know
that each had expected too much—
That each had built a myth around
the other
and cast him in a role he could not play . . .
the role of a perfect human being.

And neither could accept the imperfections
of the other.

They did not know that imperfections
are what make love possible,
for without them, there would be nothing
to magnify those qualities
that might approach perfection.
There would be no room for change,
for growth.

They did not understand
that imperfections are people . . .
and life . . .
and the world.
And they are the challenges that
make living worthwhile.

And sometimes those who really love us,
love our imperfections most of all.

I know a little girl with freckles,
and she hates them.
But to me,
she would be plain
without them.

Lilacs and Rainy Days

It was over thirty years ago and it was Spring. The sudden
roads of war machines lay muddy from the rains of early
April and trailed like dingy scars across the face of Bel-
gium's greenery; denying Spring its promise of new life,
trampling newborn plants back into the ground before they
had time to feel the sun.

It was a time when killing was in vogue, in a place
where youth and innocence and beauty all were dying.

We were being moved from one someplace to another,
riding on a truck, when suddenly I saw a little girl standing
by the roadside. She was smiling the way little girls always
smile when they have a secret they can hardly wait to tell.
She was about eight, I guessed. Her feet were bare and her
toes were digging little caves in the mud. There was a black
lace scarf on her head and her face was the face of every
child the world has ever known.

There was a small wicker basket at her side, and as we
passed, she took sprigs of lilacs from it and threw them to
us. I caught one . . . held it to my face and smelled
it . . . then looked back and waved. She was smiling as she
disappeared from view as we made a sudden turn.

She had said nothing. Yet, she had said much. With her
flowers and her face, she had told us that somewhere things
were still growing . . . that there was new life amidst the

dying . . . that there were children still . . . and laughter and music and books and make-believe and loving . . . and being loved.

For all these years I have wondered where she went that day and if the war let her grow up, and if she is alive.

And I have wished that there were some way I could let her know that the scent of lilacs . . . and rainy days in Spring . . . will forever hold a very special place in the memory of one who shared them both with her for just a passing moment . . . so very long ago.

Sweet Retrospect

We choose the moments
and the days
we would like to live again . . .
forgetting those less pleasant ones
that came before—
and after.

And these hand-picked yesterdays
of our lives,
that we recall so fondly now,

are made to seem more precious
by the interval that lies between . . .
sweeter than they were
when they were today.
They were not so important then.
The present never seems to be.
It is the present
we take for granted.
It is the past
we glorify.

The Trees

They stood so proud—
the trees—
majestic creations
of some quiet miracle
that breathed life
into a barren land.

They gave freely
of their shade,
their timber,
and their fruit,
asking naught but that
a seed be buried for
some tomorrow's need.

Now, in defeat they lie,
felled by the tools
men use
in the name of progress.
       . . . PROGRESS . . .
That omnipotent euphemism
that confuses
advancement with change
and presumes
they are the same.

Summer Lovers

Let's hold our lovely, dying summer close
and share every minute that remains,
before the winds of autumn come,
leaping
from behind a sudden cloud.

For then, it will be goodbye.
　　Goodbye to afternoons
　　we cast in bronze,
　　and barefoot trails
　　across the sand.
　　Goodbye to midnights,
　　wading through the stars
　　reflected on the water . . .
　　　　to the changing patterns
　　　　sea gulls make,
　　　　and to crimson flowers,
　　　　painted on the bay at dawn.

So love me now . . .
in this warm, together time.
Love me now . . .
and give me memories enough
to last me
through the lonely winter.

Soft Farewell

I hope there is not time
to say goodbye
when my darkness comes,
for I would not know how
to bid my loves farewell—
    or which to choose
    to share that final moment.

Which lips to kiss,
which hand to hold,
which sunset to recall,
which rose,
which song,
which season.

Please spare me the choosing.
    For I have loved so much of life—
    so much more than I have hated.

So many things,
so many ways,
so many times,
so many people.

Please let me see it
all as one
as I am leaving—
one single great adventure.

And let it embrace me
and take my breath
and close my eyes
and bid me
soft farewell.